CONTENTS

Richard II

Act 2, Scene 1

William Shakespeare (1564–1616)

This royal throne of kings, this sceptred isle,
This earth of majesty, this seat of Mars,
This other Eden, demi-paradise,
This fortress built by Nature for herself
Against infection and the hand of war,
This happy breed of men, this little world,
This precious stone set in the silver sea
Which serves it in the office of a wall
Or as a moat defensive to a house
Against the envy of less happier lands,
This blessed plot, this earth, this realm,
this England.

(1595)

All decorative pictures are captioned on page 2.

sceptred
Royal (A sceptre is a staff carried by a monarch).

seat of Mars
Home of Mars, who was the Roman god of war.

Eden
The place where God created Adam and Eve.

demi-paradise
Half a paradise, because God's original Eden is the only true paradise.

breed
Race.

office
Function.

This poetic speech comes from *Richard II*, one of William Shakespeare's history plays. It is spoken by John of Gaunt, who is King Richard II's uncle. He is proud to be English and thinks of his country as being close to perfection. As an island England is blessed by God, he says, because the sea protects it like a moat around a castle. It is the perfect home for its royal rulers. The poem is written in 'blank verse', which means there are no rhymes. Shakespeare uses beautiful images and vivid language instead.

This is the family tree of John of Gaunt. The rich liked to show they had noble ancestors, particularly if they were related to royal families.

In the play, John of Gaunt's speech is in fact criticizing Richard II, who ruled England from 1377 to 1399. However, by describing England in such proud, patriotic terms, Shakespeare would have pleased Queen Elizabeth (ruled 1558–1603) who was queen when the play was written.

Because of poor rule by kings such as Richard II, England was not a very strong country when the Tudor family came to the throne in 1485. But the reign of Elizabeth, who was the last of the Tudor monarchs, was a golden age for England. The English navy's defeat of mighty Spain in 1588 confirmed England as a great power. The 'happy breed of men' who watched Shakespeare's play would have shared Gaunt's pride in their country's success.

These beautifully carved ivory knife-handles from around 1600 show some of the kings and queens of England.

The Steel Glass

George Gascoigne (c.1525–1577)

Four estates, to serve each country soil,
The king, the knight, the peasant,
and the priest.
The king should care for all the subjects still,
The knight should fight for to defend the same,
The peasant he should labour for their ease,
And priests should pray for them
and for themselves.
But alas, such mists do bleary our eyes
And instead they do clothe themselves
with silks of strange devises.

(1576)

estates
Classes of people.

soil
Here, this means the land belonging to one nation.

subjects
The people ruled over by a king.

labour for their ease
Work hard so that life is easier for others.

bleary our eyes
Make us blind.

silks of strange devises
Clothes (and therefore roles) that do not suit them.

This extract describes the four different 'estates' or classes that made up Tudor society, and the roles they were expected to play. It says the king should rule, and his knights should defend him. Peasants should work hard to support their superiors. The priests should pray for everyone, including themselves. The poem also says that people should accept their place in society. But the last two lines complain that some people do not see this clearly, and try to play strange roles that do not suit their proper rank.

Although the four estates of Tudor society were very similar to those of medieval times, important changes had taken place. Merchants were becoming more important in society, and the peasant's life had improved. Before Tudor times, peasants had been owned by the lord of the manor. Now they were free to leave his land and work for a different lord.

Farming was the most important industry in England. This farmer and his wife are going to market to sell some of the things they have grown or made.

POET'S CORNER

George Gascoigne became a Member of Parliament in 1557 and took up the life of a courtier. But his extravagance caused him money problems, and landed him in prison. Perhaps he was living beyond his proper estate! After his release, he wanted adventure and served as a soldier in Holland fighting against the Spanish.

But the importance of loyalty to your betters was still thought to be important. Most people believed that God had chosen the king, who in turn had chosen his 'knights', or lords. Kings and lords obviously hoped people would accept their situation in life because they were at the top of society. But there were many cases of priests setting poor examples, and of peasants rebelling against their rulers.

This famous painting of a wedding feast in London shows people of different estates. The rich parade their wealth while the less rich look on or are busy in their different trades.

Hark, Hark, the Dogs do Bark

(A Tudor nursery rhyme)

Hark, hark, the dogs do bark,
The beggars are coming to town.
Some in rags and some in tags
And some in silken gowns.

Some gave them white bread,
Some gave them brown,
And some of them
gave them a good horse-whip,
And sent them out of town.

(traditional)

Hark
Listen.

tags
Respectable clothing.

This nursery rhyme describes the fears many Tudor people felt about the growing army of poor people who begged on the streets. The first part (in the present tense) gives a sense of something frightening approaching. The people in 'rags' are probably just beggars, but those in 'silken gowns' make a living as con-artists. The second part of the rhyme (in the past tense) looks back on the beggars' visit. The kindest people gave them white bread which was thought to be nicer than brown. Horse-whipping was a common punishment for those caught begging.

This is Nicholas Jennings, *a notorious Elizabethan criminal. In the left-hand picture, he is dressed as a gentleman. On the right, he is disguised as a beggar.*

I n the sixteenth century, the numbers of poor people without work grew alarmingly. Fewer people were needed to work on farms because of the increase of sheep farming – which required less labour. The price of food rose but wages did not. So the poor became even poorer.

By 1590, there were more than 10,000 homeless people wandering the countryside. In the past, the monks and friars had helped the poor. But Henry VIII had closed many of the monasteries and sold off the buildings. In 1599 a Poor Law was passed. Workhouses were set up where the poor could get help in return for work, but the rules in these places were very strict.

POET'S CORNER

Nursery rhymes were not originally meant for children. They were usually written to describe an important event or social problem. This one probably dates from Queen Elizabeth's reign. But some people think it started almost 100 years later to celebrate King William III arriving in England with Dutch supporters known as 'sea-beggars'.

This frieze from the early 1500s shows beggars receiving bread from the Church.

The Praise and Virtue of a Jail and Jailers

John Taylor (1580–1653)

In London, and within a mile I ween
There are of jails or prisons full eighteen,
And sixty whipping-posts, and stocks and cages,
Where sin with shame and sorrow
hath due wages.
For though the Tower be a castle royal,
Yet there's a prison for men disloyal,
And last it is a prison unto those
That so their sovereign or his laws oppose.

(1618)

Virtue
Goodness or benefits.

ween
Think.

stocks
A wooden frame holding
the legs of a criminal made
to sit on public display.

cages
Offenders were also put
on display in cages.

wages
Reward.

Tower
The Tower of London, which
was a castle and a prison.

sovereign
Ruler or monarch.

This poem describes the many punishments awaiting criminals in London if they broke the law. Taylor notes how many jails there are in the city – even the royal castle, the Tower of London, is a prison for traitors. He uses a religious tone typical of the Tudors, saying the punishments are a reward not just for crime, but for sin. The poem was written for ordinary people – at least, for those who could read! It contains rhyming couplets (which means each pair of lines rhymes) to make it easier to read and remember.

The Tower of London was built by William the Conqueror. In Tudor times, it was used as a prison for the most dangerous enemies of the state.

POET'S CORNER

John Taylor was a 'pamphleteer', who wrote popular, comic verses. His poems were published in hundreds of cheap pamphlets to be bought on the streets and read by ordinary people. Taylor knew a lot about London. He ran a public house there. He also worked as a waterman on the Thames. So, he was known as the Water-poet.

Tudor London was a huge city, when most other towns in England were no bigger than a small market town of today. The crime rate was rising, and as prisons increased in number so did the list of savage punishments for criminals.

Punishments were often carried out in public. Petty criminals such as pickpockets were suspended in cages, or put in the stocks and pelted with stones and rotten food. Beggars were whipped. If they continued to beg, they were branded on the forehead or had their ears and noses slit. If caught a third time, they might be hanged. The worst crime of all was to commit treason against the king. Anyone found guilty of this was thrown in the Tower of London to await execution.

People caught begging were paraded around towns and whipped, as both a punishment and a warning to others.

Satyres

Samuel Rowlands (c. 1570–1630)

He fits the humours of them in their kind,
With every month, new liveries to their mind,
A busk, a mask, a fan, a monstrous ruff,
A bolster for their buttocks, and such stuff,
More light and toyish
than the wind-blown chaff,
As though they meant
to make the Devil laugh.

(1600)

Satyres
Satire is writing that makes fun of people.

humours
Feelings or moods.

liveries
Distinctive clothes or uniforms.

busk
A bodice.

ruff
A starched, frilled collar that sticks out.

bolster
A piece of padding.

chaff
Husks of corn.

Samuel Rowlands is making fun of the Tudor 'trendies', who want to be seen in the latest fashions each month. In doing so, he leaves us a marvellous description of Tudor clothes. The poem criticizes empty-headed people, who spend all their money and time buying the tailor's latest designs in clothes. Not only are these people as worthless as husks of corn, to be blown away in the wind, but even the Devil must be laughing at how ridiculous they look.

A nd what might the trendiest Tudor gentleman have worn? First, a pair of tights, over which he pulled on short trousers called 'hose'. These were stuffed with horsehair to puff them out, and were often slashed to show expensive cloth beneath. On top he wore a shirt with broad sleeves, and a tight-fitting jacket called a 'doublet'.

This noblewoman wears an enormous ruff, which required a large amount of starch to keep it sticking out.

As for the ladies, they commonly wore a large, hooped frame beneath their skirts called a 'farthingale'. Narrow waists were popular, so women squeezed into iron corsets, or woollen ones stiffened with whalebone. On top, ladies put on silk or satin gowns. Sticky-out bottoms were fashionable, so they padded the backs of their dresses. Both men and women wore starched lace collars called 'ruffs', which were sometimes of enormous size.

Sir Philip Sidney, a famous poet, wearing a ruff with a metal collar.

POET'S CORNER

Rowlands wrote many 'satirical' poems that made fun of the silly behaviour of people. This made him many enemies. Although he was careful not to attack the rich and famous too openly, many individuals recognized themselves in his work. The authorities became so annoyed with Rowlands at one time that they ordered his writing to be burned in public!

Inviting a Friend for Supper

Ben Jonson (1572–1637)

Tonight, grave sir, both my poor house and I
Do equally desire your company:
An olive, capers, or some better salad
Ushering the mutton; with a short-legged hen
If we can get her, full of eggs, and then,
I'll tell you of more, and lie, so you will come:
Of partridge, pheasant, woodcock, of which some
May yet be there; and goodwit, if we can,
Knat, rail, and ruff too.

(1616)

grave sir
Important gentleman.

desire your company
Would like you to join us.

capers
A pickled delicacy.

Ushering
Arriving ahead of.

partridge, pheasant, woodcock, goodwit, knat, rail, ruff
These are all types of bird.

What is your favourite food? Would you like to have been invited to supper with Ben Jonson? He so desperately wants this important gentleman to come to supper that he is prepared to 'lie' about all the good food that he wishes he could give to his guest. Tudor people ate just about anything that flapped a wing. Some of the birds mentioned in the poem are now protected by law, but partridge and pheasant are still eaten today.

The rich enjoyed a range of meats, including wild boar, deer and small birds. They also ate vegetables, such as 'olives' and 'capers', though some thought of vegetables as food for peasants. Meals were served on slabs of bread called 'trenchers' and guests were often expected to bring their own knives. Spoons and cups were provided by the host.

A wealthy family at dinner.

Some recipes were very unusual. One dish, called the 'cockatrice', was made by sewing the back half of a pig on to the front half of a cockerel. 'Four-and-Twenty Blackbirds', the nursery rhyme, also describes an actual recipe! A meat pie was baked, and then live birds were placed beneath a false crust. The writer of the recipe is sure that this will give great delight to the guests!

POET'S CORNER

Ben Jonson started his working life as a bricklayer, and then became a clergyman. In 1597 he became an actor and playwright. A year later, he killed an actor in a quarrel and was sentenced to hang. But, because he was a clergyman, he was punished instead by being branded on his forehead with the letter 'M' for murderer.

A Tudor painting of game birds eaten by the rich.

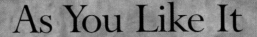

As You Like It

Act 2, Scene 7

William Shakespeare (1564–1616)

All the world's a stage,
And all the men and women merely players:
They have their exits and their entrances;
And one man in his time plays many parts,
His acts being seven ages. At first the infant,
Mewling and puking in the nurse's arms.
And then the whining school-boy,
with his satchel
And shining morning face,
creeping like a snail
Unwillingly to school.

(1599)

players
Actors.

exits, entrances
Deaths and births.

mewling, puking
Crying and being sick.

In this extract from one of his comedy plays, Shakespeare uses one of his favourite 'metaphors' – describing people's lives as the performances of actors. As we grow older we are forced to play different parts. The seven 'ages' of our lives are like the acts of a play. The first 'age' is when we are a screaming, puking baby. And did you recognize yourself in your second age, 'creeping like a snail' to school? The passage goes on to describe a lover, soldier, judge, old man and, finally, the second childhood of extreme old age!

Travelling actors give a performance at a mansion in the countryside.

POET'S

CORNER

In 1599, the theatre of Shakespeare's company, the Lord Chamberlain's Men, was threatened with closure. So, the company dismantled the theatre and rebuilt it on the other side of the Thames. The new theatre was a great success. Shakespeare, who had written the line 'All the world's a stage' called the theatre – The Globe!

The round buildings flying flags at the bottom-left of this beautiful painting of London are the theatres.

Watching plays had always been popular, but during the reign of Queen Elizabeth the English theatre burst into life. This was not to everybody's liking. Despite their popularity, actors were thought of as little more than rogues. Religious groups such as the Puritans even tried to have the theatres closed down. For their own safety, actors banded together in companies under the protection of powerful nobles.

Because theatres were thought to be rough, dangerous places, women were not allowed to become actors. So their parts had to be played by boys dressed in women's clothes. The audience was used to this, and it made people laugh even more when the women characters in a play such as *As You Like It* disguised themselves as men!

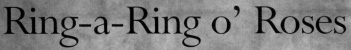

Ring-a-Ring o' Roses

(A Tudor nursery rhyme)

Ring-a-ring o' roses
A pocketful of posies
Atishoo! Atishoo!
We all fall down.

Adieu, Farewell Earth's Bliss

Thomas Nashe, 1567–1601

Rich men trust not in wealth,
Gold cannot buy you health;
Physic himself must fade,
All things to end are made,
The plague full swift goes by;
I am sick, I must die:
Lord, have mercy on us.

(1591)

posies
Small bunches of sweet-smelling flowers.

Adieu
Goodbye.

Physic
A doctor.

full swift
Very quickly.

N o disease was as greatly feared as the plague. The 'ring o' roses' describes the dark swellings called 'buboes' that appeared on a victim's body. Sufferers began to sneeze violently and finally would 'fall down' dead. Some people carried posies to disguise the stench of disease. Nashe's religious poem warns that riches are no protection against the epidemic. Many sufferers wrote a warning on their doors: 'Lord, have mercy on us!' All they could hope was that God might take pity on them.

Bubonic plague was known as the Black Death after the black spots that appeared on the victim's skin. Once the plague arrived, it spread like wildfire. The disease was actually caught through the bite of a rat-flea. Once the infection was in the bloodstream, the sufferer was likely to be dead within three days.

Londoners flee from the plague. Death appears in the background, ready to strike.

Some doctors believed the atmosphere was poisoned by the disease, and suggested burning barrels of tar in the streets to clean the air. Others suggested weird and wonderful cures such as opening a vein to let bad blood out, or telling their patients to eat the shavings from the head of an executed criminal mixed with a little hedgehog grease. If the disease didn't kill you, the cure probably would!

POET'S CORNER

Thomas Nashe was born in Lowestoft. He was the son of a clergyman. Nashe travelled widely in France and Italy before finally settling in London as a writer in 1588. Much of his work attacked the Puritans, whom he disliked a great deal. After the performance of one of his plays, the theatre was closed and Nashe was thrown in prison.

This Tudor pomander was filled with scented herbs and spices. This was believed to keep away disease as well as unpleasant smells.

Epithalamion

Edmund Spenser (c.1552–1599)

Let no deluding dreams, nor dreadful sights,
Make sudden sad afrights,
Nor let house fires nor lightning's helpless harms,
Nor let the Puck nor other evil sprites,
Nor let mischievous witches with their charms,
Nor let hobgoblins' names whose sense we see not
Frighten us with things that be not.
Let not the screech owl nor the stork be heard,
Nor the night raven that still deadly yells,
Nor damned ghosts called up with mighty spells.
Nor grisly vultures make us once afeared.

(1597)

Epithalamion
An 'epithalamium' is a song or poem written for a wedding.

deluding
Deceiving.

afrights
Frights, things that scare us.

Puck, sprites
Naughty spirits.

hobgoblins
Mischievous elves.

grisly
Causing horror or terror.

afeared
Frightened.

Edmund Spenser creates an eerie feeling in this extract. The rhythms and rhymes, and the repeated words at the beginnings of lines, give a sense of a spell being cast. There are all sorts of symbols of black magic listed – spirits, witches, ghosts, frogs, and birds with superstitions attached to them. But the poem says that we should not be frightened by evil spirits such as 'Puck' and 'hobgoblins'. It is as if the poem is casting its own spell, to keep away such evil charms and influences.

Edmund Spenser, who knew all about evil influences. In 1585, his house in Ireland was burned to the ground and he was forced to flee to London.

In Tudor times, people were very superstitious. It was difficult to explain why certain things happened – why houses caught fire or why a cow suddenly stopped giving milk. So, people blamed these events on evil influences.

A number of laws made it a crime to practise magic. Between 1582 and 1682, over 1,000 people were executed as witches in England and Wales. Many of them were lonely old women. Pets such as black cats were believed to be the witches' 'familiars' or spirits (like the birds in Spenser's poem). Some women were tried in courts, and many were tortured to make them confess. They were plunged into lakes on ducking stools, or 'floated' in rivers. If they drowned they were mere mortals after all, and were innocent!

This engraving shows three executed witches and their familiars. The witches were hanged at Chelmsford in 1589.

POET'S CORNER

Edmund Spenser was born in London, and worked in Ireland – which was ruled over by the English kings and queens. He bought a large country house there, in Cork, where he wrote *The Fairie Queen*, a famous poem in praise of Queen Elizabeth. *Epithalamion* was written to celebrate Spenser's wedding in 1594.

Orchestra

Sir John Davies (1569–1626)

❧

Only the earth does stand forever still,
Her rocks remove not nor her mountains meet;
Although some wits enriched with a learning skill
Say heaven stands firm
and that the earth does fleet
And swiftly turneth underneath their feet.
Yet though the earth is ever steadfast seen,
On her broad breast has dancing ever been.

(1596)

remove
Move from one place to another.

wits
Clever people.

fleet
Move quickly.

Steadfast
Unmoving.

Almost all of us have written our address giving the name of the street, town and country – and ending with 'The Universe'. We call all the stars and planets that exist the 'universe', and this extract from Sir John Davies' poem is about how Tudor people understood the universe they lived in. The poem takes the view that the earth is fixed and stationary, and the sun and planets revolve around it. But it notes how 'wits', or scientists, say that in fact the earth is moving. It is fascinating to read a poem written at a moment when a new scientific idea was still being argued about.

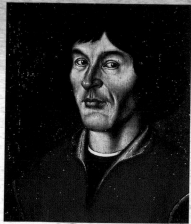

Nicholas Copernicus, the Polish monk who proved that the earth revolved around the sun.

The sixteenth century was a time of incredible discoveries. Scientists were just beginning to understand how the world and the universe worked. About fifty years before this poem was written, a famous astronomer called Copernicus made a very important discovery. By studying the stars, he came up with an idea that shocked many people. He said that the earth was in fact revolving around the sun, and that the sun was the real centre of our system of planets.

Teachers in the Church were outraged. They taught that God had created the earth as the centre of the universe – and if you could travel up you would pass the planets and the angels, and eventually reach heaven. Now a scientist was daring to say we were not the centre of everything. But Copernicus was right!

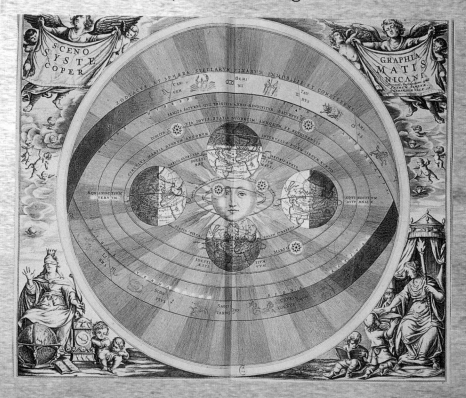

A painting showing the universe described by Copernicus, with the sun at the centre.

The Winning of Cales

Thomas Doloney (1543–1600)

Long the proud Spaniard advanced to conquer us
Threatening our country with fire and sword,
Often preparing their navy most sumptuous,
With all the provision that Spain could afford,
Dub, a dub, dub, thus strikes their drummes,
Tan ta ra ra, tan ta ra ra,
English men comes.

Unto Cales cunningly came we most happily
Where the king's navy securely did ride,
Being upon their backs,
piercing their butts of sacks,
Ere that the Spaniard our coming described.
Tan ta ra ra, ra, English men comes,
Bounce abounce, bounce abounce,
Off went our guns.

(1596)

sumptuous
Rich and costly.

provision
Food and equipment.

Cales
*Another name for Cadiz,
a port in Spain.*

butts of sacks
Barrels of Spanish wine.

Ere that
Before.

Spain was the richest country in Europe during the reign of Elizabeth I. The first verse of this ballad records Spain's role as England's rich and deadly enemy. The second verse describes a famous raid made by the English navy against the Spanish port of Cadiz. With its many rhymes and strong rhythm, the ballad was easy to sing. It also uses 'onomatopoeia' – which means words that impersonate sounds, such as the 'Dub, a dub, dub' of a drum.

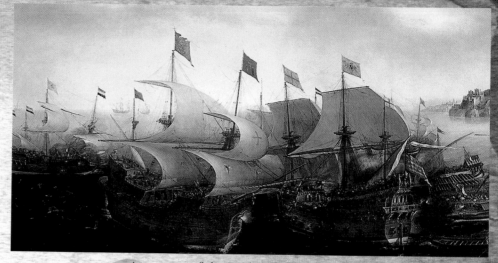

A painting of the English fleet attacking the Spanish ships in the harbour at Cadiz.

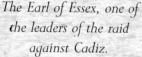

The Earl of Essex, one of the leaders of the raid against Cadiz.

Throughout Queen Elizabeth's long reign, England and Spain quarrelled fiercely over such matters as religion, empire and control of the seas. In 1588, Philip of Spain sent the Armada, a huge fleet of ships, to invade England. But it was defeated in one of England's most famous naval victories.

As the ballad shows, the two countries remained at war after the Armada battle. The raid at Cadiz was another great success for the English. Their own armada of over 100 ships was led by Sir Walter Raleigh and Elizabeth's young favourite, the Earl of Essex. Each time the Spanish guns fired, the English trumpeters replied to them with a fanfare: 'Tan ta ra ra!' As the ballad suggests, the English fleet surprised the Spaniards and famously captured Cadiz.

A Religious Use of Tobacco

Robert Wisdome (c.1515—1568)

And when the smoke ascends on high,
Think thou beholds the vanity
Of worldly stuff, gone with a puff,
Thus think, then drink tobacco.

But when the pipe grows foul within,
Think of thy soul defiled with sin.
And that the fire, doth it require:
Thus think, then drink tobacco.

The ashes that are left behind,
May serve to put thee still in mind
That into dust, return thou must:
Thus think, then drink tobacco.

(c.1560)

ascends
Rises.

thou
You.

vanity
Pride.

defiled
Stained, made impure.

This is a religious poem which makes its point by comparing a person's life to the act of smoking tobacco. The first verse says that just as tobacco turns to smoke, so our material luxuries will quickly vanish. The second explains that when a person does wrong, his soul becomes dirty like a tobacco pipe – the mention of fire is a frightening reminder of hell. Finally, Wisdome uses the image of the ashes that are left in the pipe to remind the reader that one day we all must die and be buried in the earth.

As Europeans began to explore the world in their sailing ships they came across many animals and plants they had never seen before. One such plant was tobacco, the dried leaves of which the Native Americans smoked. Christopher Columbus had brought tobacco seeds back to Europe, and English colonists in America began growing the plant for export.

This Native American priest was painted in the sixteenth century by John White, one of the first English settlers in America.

Today we know that smoking can cause serious health problems. But in Tudor times, the fad quickly caught on. Some people even claimed that tobacco could cure illnesses, such as the plague. Others hated the weed, blaming it for making smokers lazy good-for-nothings. James I, who became king after the death of Elizabeth I in 1603, even wrote a book about how much he hated the evil habit.

This engraving from the time of James I shows three gentlemen smoking their pipes. Note the strange spelling of 'smoking'.

To the Virginian Voyage

Michael Drayton (1563–1631)

Britons, you stay too long.
Quickly aboard bestow you,
And with a merry gale
Swell your stretched sail,
With vows as strong,
As the winds that blow you.

And cheerfully at sea,
Success you still entice,
To get the pearl and gold,
And ours to hold,
  Virginia
Earth's only paradise.

(1606)

bestow you
Take your place.

vows
Promises.

entice
Tempt.

Virginia
A region of America claimed by English colonists.

This poem is asking for people in Britain to sail for the colonies in America. The first verse scolds British adventurers for being too cautious. The second tempts them with the treasure that is rumoured to await explorers in the New World. It is interesting to compare Drayton's last line – 'Earth's only paradise' – with Shakespeare's description of England in our first poem: 'This other Eden, demi-paradise.' To avoid upsetting the Church, both write of an earthly or 'demi' paradise rather than the true paradise of heaven.

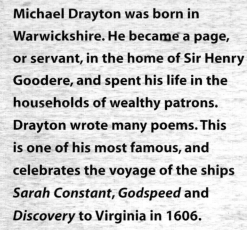

Michael Drayton was born in Warwickshire. He became a page, or servant, in the home of Sir Henry Goodere, and spent his life in the households of wealthy patrons. Drayton wrote many poems. This is one of his most famous, and celebrates the voyage of the ships *Sarah Constant*, *Godspeed* and *Discovery* to Virginia in 1606.

This early map of Virginia shows the Native American leader, Powhatan, who befriended some of the early English settlers and helped them to survive.

From the fifteenth century onwards, European sailors made use of recent improvements in shipbuilding and ocean navigating to find new routes to the Spice Islands, east of India. Adventurers were tempted to make these dangerous voyages by the promise of finding riches to trade. The excitement of expeditions to new lands gripped people just as space flights to the planets fascinate us today.

The National Lottery is not a new idea. This engraving shows the drawing of the 'Great Standing Lottery for Virginia' in 1615. The lottery raised money for the expensive business of setting up and running the colony.

Voyages through uncharted seas to unknown lands changed forever the way Europeans understood their world. They discovered the globe was much bigger than they had imagined, and that all the oceans were connected. Most surprising of all, was the discovery of a huge continent west of Europe, which they called America. English explorers claimed a part of it – naming it Virginia after Elizabeth, the Virgin Queen. The colony provided a new inspiration for the poets of the day.

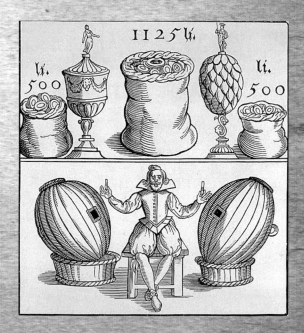

GLOSSARY

Difficult words from the verse appear alongside each poem. This glossary explains words used in the main text. The page numbers are given so that you can study the glossary then see how the words have been used.

armada (p. 25) A large fleet of ships, especially that sent by Spain against England in 1588.

astronomer (p. 23) Someone who studies the stars and planets.

ballad (p. 24) A simple song that tells a story in several verses.

balladeer (p. 25) Someone who writes ballads.

Black Death (p. 19) Plague, particularly the epidemic that swept Europe in the fourteenth century.

branded (p. 11) Scarred with a red-hot piece of iron.

Bubonic Plague (p. 19) A highly contagious, deadly disease, which takes its name from the 'buboe' which appeared on its victims' bodies.

capers (p. 15) The pickled buds of a shrub, often used in a sauce.

Catholic (p. 27) The part of the Christian Church with the Pope as its head.

colonists (p. 27) Settlers in a foreign country who still obey their original king or queen.

con-artists (p. 8) People who swindle or trick others out of their money.

corsets (p. 13) Tight-fitting garments designed to press the stomach in.

courtier (p. 7) Someone who regularly attends the court of a king or queen.

cudgel (p. 23) A short, thick stick or club used as a weapon.

eerie (p. 20) Scary, gloomy, strange.

empire (p. 25) Countries around the world under the control of one ruler.

epidemic (p. 18) A disease that affects many members of a community.

export (p. 27) The sale of goods to a foreign country.

extract (p. 16) Part of a poem or story.

fad (p. 27) A trend or fashion.

family tree (p. 5) A chart showing the ancestors and members of a family.

fanfare (p. 25) A short blast of trumpets.

favourite (p. 25) Someone at court shown special favour by a king or queen.

friars (p. 9) Monks who belong to particular religious orders.

frieze (p. 9) A decoration painted on a wall.

game birds (p. 15) Birds that are hunted for sport or food.

Lord Chamberlain (p. 5) A royal official who used to give out licences to companies allowing them to perform plays.

manor (p. 7) A country estate owned by a rich nobleman.

medieval (p. 7) The period of history from 1066 to 1485, between the Norman Conquest and the rule of the Tudors.

merchants (p. 7) People who make their money by buying and selling goods, especially goods from abroad.

metaphors (p. 16) The use of one image (for example, a stage) to represent another (for example, the world).

monasteries (p. 9) The buildings where monks live.

navigating (p. 29) Directing the course of a ship.

New World (p. 28) A popular term for America in the sixteenth century.

noble (p. 5) Belonging to the upper classes.

notorious (p. 9) Very well known, usually for the wrong reasons.

page (p. 29) A young man who is employed as a servant working for a nobleman.

pamphlet (p. 11) A cheap leaflet, usually about an issue of current interest.

pamphleteer (p. 11) A writer of pamphlets.

patriotic (p. 5) Very proud of your country.

patrons (p. 29) People who give their support and protection to someone else.

peasants (p. 7) Workers on the land, who were among the poorest members of society.

plague (p. 18) A terrible disease, especially one believed to be sent by God. Particularly bubonic or pneumonic plague.

Protestant (p. 27) The part of the Christian Church that broke away from the Roman Catholic Church in the fifteenth century.

Puritans (p. 17) An organization of Protestants with very strict religious beliefs.

rebelling (p. 7) Fighting against the authorities.

satirical (p. 13) Making fun of people's behaviour.

second childhood (p. 16) The time when someone elderly behaves like a child because of senility.

sermon (p. 27) A speech or lesson given by a clergyman from the church pulpit.

traitors (p. 10) People who are disloyal to their king or queen.

treason (p. 11) Plotting against your own king or queen.

trendies (p. 12) People who try to be fashionable.

uncharted (p. 29) Undiscovered, not marked on maps.

vivid (p. 4) Clear and intense, giving a very powerful impression.

waterman (p. 11) A taxi driver, except his taxi was a boat on the river.

weed (p. 27) A slang name for tobacco.

whalebone (p. 13) Hard but elastic substance from inside a whale's jaw, used for stiffening items such as corsets.

workhouses (p. 9) Public buildings where poor people can receive lodgings in exchange for work.

BOOKS TO READ

A Children's English History in Verse by Kenneth Baker (ed.) (Faber, 1999)

Life in Tudor Times (Cambridge Primary History) by Christine Counsell (Cambridge, 1997)

The New Oxford Book of Children's Verse by Neil Philip (ed.) (Oxford, 1996)

Tudor Odours (Smelly Old History) by Mary J. Dobson (Oxford, 1997)

Tudor Times by Neil Tonge and Peter Hepplewhite (Folens, 1996)

INDEX

Numbers in **bold** refer
to pictures and captions.